"Echoes of Verses"

Vidya Mathews

BookLeaf
Publishing

India | USA | UK

Presentation by *BookLeaf Publishing*

Web: www.bookleafpub.com

E-mail: info@bookleafpub.com

ISBN: 9789360949426

First edition 2024

DEDICATION

I dedicate this book to:

The past that shaped me, the present that nurtures me, and the future that awaits me.

My parents, who planted the seed of knowledge in my mind and nurtured it.

All those who pick up this book: thank you for giving my words a chance. May you find the courage, joy, and love contained within these pages.

My dearest Jen, the one who fills my heart with joy each and every day. You are the melody to my lyrics, the inspiration behind my words, and the light that guides my pen.

This collection of poetry is a birthday gift to you, a way to let you know the infinite ways you enrich my life.

With love always,

Vidya Mathews

ACKNOWLEDGEMENT

To my dearest daughter,

As I pen down these words, I am filled with a profound sense of gratitude for the light you have brought into my life. Your unwavering support, boundless love, and innate wisdom have been constant sources of inspiration as I embarked on this poetic journey.

You have taught me the true meaning of empathy, patience, and resilience. Your gentle spirit and compassionate heart have touched the lives of all who know you, and I am endlessly proud to call you my daughter.

In moments of doubt and uncertainty, you have been my rock, offering encouragement and understanding with unwavering grace. Your belief in me has fueled my creative spirit and propelled me forward, even when the path seemed uncertain.

This collection of poetry may look childish as some of them were written even before you were born. This collection is as much yours as it is mine, for it bears the imprint of your love and

the echoes of your laughter. I wouldn't have
re-opened my diary of inner feelings, had you
not encouraged me.
Thank you for being my muse, my confidante,
and my greatest supporter.

With all my love,

Mom

PREFACE

In the tapestry of existence, our lives are woven together with threads of experience, emotion, and reflection. "Echoes of Verses: Poetic Reflections on Life's Journey" invites you to embark on a lyrical and non-lyrical exploration of the human thoughts and feelings—a journey through the depths of the heart and the vast expanse of the soul.

Within these pages, you will encounter a symphony of emotions, each poem a melody that resonates with the rhythms of life. From the gentle whispers of love to the thunderous echoes of loss, these verses offer glimpses into the universal truths that bind us all together.

As the poet, I have endeavoured to capture the essence of the shared humanity with honesty and empathy. Each word is a brushstroke on the canvas of existence, painting portraits of love, longing, joy, sorrow, and resilience.

I invite you, dear reader, to wander through these poetic landscapes—to pause, reflect, and find solace in the beauty of language and the power of expression. May these echoes of existence serve as companions on your own journey of self-discovery and enlightenment.

With heartfelt gratitude,

Vidya Mathews

INDEX

Realization

The world with all its beauty
Calls me for some other duty
Life which I wished was like a feather
For which I didn't have to bother
Without a second glance
God gave me another chance

Though it looked light as a card
To bear, it was a little hard

A bit longer did it take me to realize
The way I had chosen wasn't very wise

But what could regrets do
Coz life is only one not two
As I craved for ultimate peace
It felt like God came to my release

That's when I felt, He sent me with a purpose
To follow the Word of God is what matters
He called me for a bigger Duty
To enlighten the world about God's beauty

The stone that paused my thought

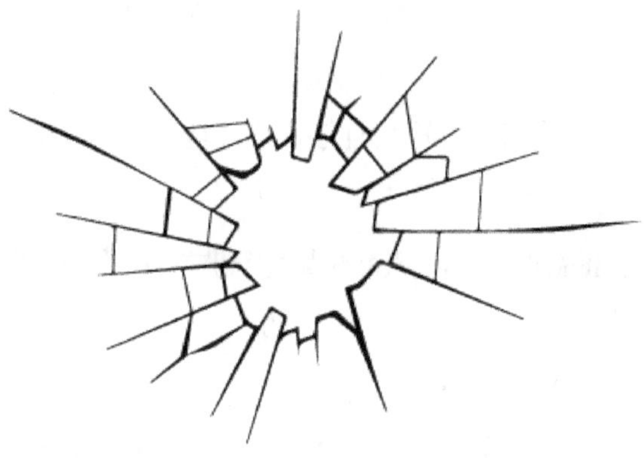

I looked into the rearview mirror today n' felt...
life was slipping away.
I don't know whether anything changed for the
world
But the world for sure had changed for me.

It was all calm till one stone hit the windshield
The loud shattering noise almost burst my ear
Hue and cry, sticks and stones from far and near
Tore the darkness of the night into red-hot amber

Hatred took over not only me but this lane, this
alley
and covered the whole city making it ugly

Is this the same peaceful road I crossed daily?

I looked into the rearview mirror; the night was
still not over...
Was it for only me or everyone? I started to ponder,
Pain and fear made me realize ...life had been taken
away.
A small stone from nowhere changed my life
forever.

I looked into the rearview mirror, moving away
from the clamour
Searching for the hand that hurled the stone and was
unaware...
How my heart was pierced, and my thoughts got
clouded,

Asking each nameless face in the night dark and
cold...
Are you the one who flung that stone like an
armour?

Face smeared in blood, covered with shattered glass,
still holding the stone...
What made them hurl this stone towards me? I
thought.
Will I feel safe again, in my lane as old times?
I questioned.
Fearful feelings made the darkness of the night
darker
Hesitant questions got burnt in the fire of fear and
hatred lingered in my mind
As I continued to look into the rearview mirror...

Paint your Memories

Life is a confluence of moments, filled with agony
and bliss
It is an odyssey from birth to death, you need to
choose from that n' this,

It's a choice to wisely to wait for every moment or
search for a destination unknown,
To take off with ardour, or to stare with remorse
In this Book of Life, you can choose in, what needs to
be printed as your memoirs

Life is a puzzle to which there is no answer.
The only purpose is to solve and spread the victorious
smiles.

This life is an ocean deep, t'will let you sail many
times, sink at other times,
There'll be countless challenges in the abyss, you'd
have to choose some and let some miss

Canvas of life, comes only in white;
Choose the colours on the palette, and paint it all
bright

Dance to the tune of life, as if no one is watching,
Don't be afraid of the contest unknown, with a
Smile on your lips, sparkle in your eyes
Waltz a few steps, swing on some beats, Hip-hop on
others, that is the lesson of life.

Colours of Lyfe

In the journey of life, every experience paints us
with a new colour
Dismal, gutsy, gloomy, joyous this journey is full of
countless colours.

Golden rays of the Sun to start with vigour,
white beaming moonlight to slow us into slumber,

The blue hustle and bustle of work, with the yellow
hope of tomorrow
The black difficulties of life, each moment creates a
rainbow of harmony

As the stream of time continues to flow up and
down from hills n' vales
Every moment gets redecorated and repainted with a
new hue.

From one's birth, a new form of life, protected by a
soft pink mother's love,
Nurtured by father's tough love, coated in deep red
and brown hard work,

The essence of life, the combination of colours of
love and relationships,
A team of green and purple friends walk along with
us on this journey,
Along with our family and friends, we easily strut
over life's joys and sorrows together.

No matter what happens, whether we win or lose...just
keep learning
We are and will be coated with many colours,

Don't forget to enjoy each one of them as you pass
Weave a new story with all the colours be it dark,
dull, vibrant or loud just step on, make colourful
footprints of every moment of your life

Passion in the Pale Sunshine.

At times, when pale sunshine sneaks into the sky
dark and grey,
Rays of the sun which once were alive and with many
colours play,
Gets sedated, gloomy and blurry with each passing
day.
This journey forever seems stuck at sea

With each cold gale, the colour of life fades.
Sunshine also becomes alien and ebbs into Hades
When the wizened sunlight weakens into darkness
Stepping towards its new abode, the "grave".

Look beyond the dark clouds into bursting rays of
bright new sunshine.
Fire up the passion to climb out of the crypt n' get
closer to the warm sun,
Power the weak wings with the fuel of the desire to
fly,
Take a new Angelus flight, with positivity and new
enthusiasm.

Memories of Sophia

Memories of Sophia, my alma mater, a name that is my pride.
An inspiration that continues to reside in my mind,
Haven of knowledge that instils constant search.
An ocean of thoughts, a flight of dreams,
A stream of ideology, the one which makes my heart feel limitless.

My Life's journey undoubtedly started here,
Learning together, indulging in a new action every day,

The stream of knowledge forever flows here, this
culture still nurtures us all
The harmony that accords to all who crossed this
stream
Sophia has always been the reason for what I am
today

The land of Sophia is,
the grandeur of knowledge sports and music
Love and support, that has let me win over every
arduous journey,
Where the meaning of survival is courage with
companions.
Sharing, supporting and taking bold actions every
day,

My alma mater Sophia is a unique school of dreams.
Where the path to excellence is always open and
constant.
The atmosphere there is full of grace and reverence

Helping me reach new heights and break the glass
ceiling,
I am who I am, 'cause of what I have received from
this unique heritage.

Tunes of life

In life's grand symphony the sweet tune echoes
through time and space
Soaring the clouds of dreams, I find my place.
Decorating moments with a tint of light,
With every breath, a new rhythm unfolds,
A dance of moments, where joy and sorrow are told
The light of the sun rises o'er every day,
In the vibrant journey of days, months and years
Pursuing new aims and destinations,
In this journey of discovery, I roam and explore,
In the quest, I take a flight of dreams.
Unravelling life's secrets, and finding more

Every moment filled with sweetness,
The sweetness of happiness smiles from the skies.
Smiles now reside in the heart again,
In the beauty of life, I find my voice,
A song of gratitude that echoes with every choice.
With every step, a new path unfolds,
A journey of wonder, where love never grows old.

Boy that's me

In the dry brown desert, there boldly does stray,
With hair a mess, and breaking the rules each day.

A boy's spirit, ardent, wild and free to play,
Her laughter echoes through the dunes reaching the
seas far away.

No frills, no dolls, no kitchen sets could hold her at
bay,

From flouncing on dusty fields, running, fighting
to seize the day.

Scraped-up elbows, donning dusty garbs, she would
proudly sway
Look at her grit, all set to conquer mountain roads,
come what may.

Her mirth louder than church bells chime to tell,
As she climbs walls and trees, reaching for the sky to
compel.

Her heart, untamed, with will so strong, devoid of
fear to quell,

In her world, it is an adventure far and near to
dwell.

From dawn 'til dusk, she chases the sun's warm ray,

Riding horses her tomboy heart is forever spun to stay.

Scraped-up knees and lofty dreams so grand to display,

She's here to write her destiny and conquer the world with her own way

It's been years of watching the tomboy grow to thrive
She is still the same as shining memories alive.
Still going strong, fierce, wild yet funny to survive,
O Boy, that's me, the tomboy, right here, within me,
in my heart, soul, and mind, who continues to thrive.

Brew

Right in the calm, quiet dawn, a ritual sweet,
Aromatic whispers with swirling steam,
Bedside brew is an awakening treat,
Aha!!! Life's simple joys in a cup's gleam.

In this ritual of brewing, I find a metaphor,
An alchemy of transformation, both within and
without,
As the aroma rises, it speaks of beginnings,
And the courage to embrace change, without a doubt.

Squeezing through the hustle of morn, with a cup of
glee,

I take a moment, just for me,
In that soothing ritual, I find my calm,
A pause in the chaos, like a healing balm.

In this ritual of steaming cup of my fragrant brew,
I receive comfort n' warmth in a cosy nook,
Amidst the loud shouts and screams a few,
A moment of calm, in this busy life's book

When the lethargic noon wraps around, I take a sip
of my brew,
Aromas wrap around, warming me through,
In that steaming cup, my dreams come alive,
Giving me a rush of strength, as through the day I
strive.

In this ritual of sipping the motivating n'
stimulating brew,
I discover not just warmth, but presence profound,
For in the cup's embrace, I renew,
The sanctuary of self, in which I am found.

Enjoying the sunset I sip my tea, Just before the dark
sky and the stars,
aide-memoire of the simple pleasures of life,
I am reminded that even in our darkest hours,
There is always a moment of peace in every cup.

In this ritual of steam's ascent, I hear a whispered
tale,
Of journeys taken and dreams unfurled,
In the brew, morn eve or night I find not just
warmth,
But the promise of strength, calm and hope,
un-whirled.

Spring of lyfe!!!

This spring of lyfe…
Let our days glow radiantly n' engulf the dark and
dreary wintery lowlight.
Let's bloom like new buds that spread into colourful
flowers bold and bright,
That fills the earth with sweet aromas and creates the
untold beauteous sight.
Like a tree of hope that stands taller and regains its
colour and vibrant might,

Let our stems and offshoots stretch towards the sky
like a majestic knight.

This spring of lyfe…
Like the birds, butterflies and bees that hop, skip and
play,
Let's add colour, songs and buzz to the sunshine,
making every day a joyous day.
Filling sweet melodies in the air that are loud n'
clear,
Just like their tweets and buzz, devoid of fear, let's
be heard far and near.

Let us be the warm breeze that carries whispers of new
life and hope,
Liberating the world from the cuffs of frosty nights,
making everyone elope;
Closer to the Sun, which awakens Mother Nature and
makes everything glow
With this Hope and vigour, let's melt the snow of
despair into rivers that dance and flow.

Smile Unseen

In that passing glance, a smile unfurls,
A brief bond, hearts entwine,
A moment shared, across two worlds,
In a stranger's smile, love's divine.

In that early rush, amidst the crowd,
A stranger's smile so pure and proud,
That funny gesture somehow feels right
Lifting spirits, day turned bright,

In that stranger's smile, a trace of grace,
Reminding me of our shared human race,
In brief encounters, solace found,
Familiarity in whispers unbound.

In that ephemeral smile of a passing stranger,
An affinity, a touch that makes you feel safer,
A smile that births another like a mystery,
Fills us with compassion that makes us whole, even if
it is momentary

21st Mile

Together we chatter, together we cackle
Together we wrestle, together we quarrel
Together we giggle, together we holler
Together we utter, together we mutter
We talk on matters, as vast as the sky
Words we use are as cold as snowy peaks quite high,
At times these words do get hotter than the sun
We share everything, and the never-ending stories
are fun

If one of us gets even a li'l less than our half, We
squabble till we are done,
We almost kill each other during our nasty bouts
When Mom interferes, we unite as one without any
doubts
All this and a lot more I have to say
Without you, I wouldn't be so happy any day
In my life, You are the only one
You can be definitely compared to none
As you enter the 21st year of your life
You may have to pass through new stress and strife
To churn the best out of you
You will cut through it with your grit and get your
due
Just remember you are the best
You will come out successful in this life's test.

Autumn's Whisper

As I see the crimson leaves, gently sway to play,
Nature's palette, creates a vibrant spree each day
Autumn's breeze, whizzes through my hair to dance
and sway,

Whispers to me the change, and I go wild and and
seize the day
In that passing moment, under the shadow of the
sunlight's gleam,

Memories swarm, as I walk off the streets busy theme
The whispering sound of the leaves, under my feet's
gentle beam
Creates a profound melody along with a lovely
peaceful dream

I hear the rustle of autumn leaves, en-route to a
brand new place,
I now hear nature's song, the melody of
memories,With a smiling face.
What made me who I am, in the crunch of life's
pursuit and frantic pace,
Are these moments of joy and pain, ecstasy and
miseries in a designated space.
Amidst the trees, walking through woods so tall and
green,

Enjoying the breeze, amidst the rustle of livelihoods
serene.

In that autumn air, so pristine, crisp, clear and
clean,
I find solace and peace in the beauty of this time of
year's sheen

As I stride slowly in the forest, underneath my my
feet's soft tread,
I hear the leaves crunch, in a rhythmic beat that's
echoed ahead.
In that crisp embrace, I find my cheer and a heart
that's light and spread,
As I walk through the lifeless autumn leaves,
I am reminded of the cycle of life and death,
There is always the promise of renewal, in every
breath.

My Inner Child's Laughter

Untainted and lively, with a joyful sound,
Naivety dancing on my life's stage,
As light-hearted laughter in me echoes, I feel love is found,
Every chortle in me breaks society's boundless cage.
In my heart, a child is always at play,
Her laughter rings out, as the light of day,
Makes every moment relaxed, pure and free,
I rediscovered joy, as the child in me innocently glee.
The purity of my child's laughter, when I hear,

It does not just bring innocent joy, but wisdom
profound,
For in the simplicity, devoid of fear,
Lies the essence of living, unbound
In the laughter of a child, I hear echoes,
Of innocence and joy, of dreams yet to unfold,
A reminder to embrace the present moment,
And cherish the wonder, as we grow old.

Ray of Dawn

Golden hues of early morn's first kiss,
Painting the heavens in hues so bright and bold,
A tender touch, a minute of bliss,
In dawn's embrace, secrets are unveiled and told.

At the break of day, when the sky ignites,
As I witness the sunrise, an astounding sight,
In that unique glow, I find my verve,
A reminder of the hope, and energy I deserve.

As dawn breaks, painting the sky ablaze,

In the hues of red and purple, I see the birth of
another day,
But a metaphor for resilience, in the face of night's
maze,
And the courage to embrace change, come what may.

With each sunrise, I witness a rebirth,
A reminder that darkness always yields to light,
In the colours of dawn, I see not just beauty,
But the promise of strength to beat the gloomy
night.

With each new day, I am prompted,
Of the infinite possibilities that lie ahead,
A note to me that every moment is a chance,
To begin anew, and rewrite the script of my life.

Starry Night

In the vast expanse of the night sky,
I think of the mysteries of the universe,
Each twinkling star is a reminder of infinity,
Understanding the relation of every sonnet and
verse.

As I walk along the starlit path,
I am reminded of the journey of the soul,
A reminder that even in the darkest of nights,

There is always a light to guide us home.

Looking at the limitless cosmos, I ponder,
Not just the beauty of a starlit sky,
But the insignificance of my worries, asunder,
And the connection between all, by and by.

Amidst the dark, a glittering sky,
Constellations whisper ancient tales,
In each twinkle, dreams do fly,
Night's canvas, I wonder how it prevails.

Glimmering trail of a celestial guide,
Stardust scattered, in the dark night's embrace,
In the starlit path, dreams all over far and wide,
A journey through time and space.

Underneath the stars, on a quiet night,
I gaze up at the sky, filled with delight,
In those twinkling lights, I find my way,
A sense of wonder, in the Milky Way.

In the dead of night, under the starry sky,
I walk a path, where dreams can fly,
In those distant stars, I find my guide,
A beacon of hope, where I confide.

A Book's Embrace

The aroma of the old paper, on which you can read
each written line,
Ignites a fire within my heart and a spark that makes
me shine.
With each page of trial and triumph, it adds a
symphony to my life song
Guided by prose, and inspired by poetry, I journey
along,

As pages turn, a new world gets revealed
with ink-stained dreams and journeys blue,
With a warm book's embrace, hearts get healed,
and the universe within makes a new stimulated
you.

In the arms of literature, I find my freedom,
A timeless refuge, a haven of peace.
The embrace of a book, where troubles dissolve, and
worries sweet and serene,
In those written words, I find my escape,
A journey of imagination, in every scene.

In the pages of a book, I find refuge,
A reminder that even in the darkest of times,
Within the pages of well-worn books, I discover not
just stories, but wisdom's scroll
There is always a story to guide us and remind us that
we are not alone.
In this journey of the heart and soul, towards
greatness and wholeness goal.

New Day's Promise

As the sun rises, painting the sky's canvas anew,
In hues of vibrant yellow, orange, purple and blue,
I greet the day, with a hopeful view,
In that fresh beginning, I find my way,
A chance to start afresh, come what may.

Rosy dawn, till horizon aglow,
A new day's vow, for dreams to grow,
A canvas of hope, a beating heart
The morning dew's tender kiss,
On petals fresh. O mother nature what a bliss!

With each dawn's first light, I discern,
For in the day's promise, I yearn
In the gentle whispers of dawn's first light,
Not just a new beginning, but redemption's call,
To awaken to the possibility, in each rise and fall.

Where dreams take flight,
Hope fades away the darkness of night,
Of second chances, hearts at ease.
The past recedes, the future unfurls,
In every dawn, hope gently swirls.

The promise lingers, steadfast,
To seize the day, with courage bright,
To blissfully dance with joy, in the morning's light.
For in its promise, we find our way, to live each new
day.
So, let us greet the dawn with cheer,
Embrace the day, free from fear,

Gentle You

Gentle you, who cast upon me your gaze,
That soft and tender smile sets my soul ablaze,
Passion's fire burns from yours to my heart,
Be it a dream or life we cannot ever be apart.

A pearl of beauty, pristine and pure,
Eyes that twinkle, with intense love they assure,
Early in the morn, like a prayer you gently rise,
Calms me as dawn's dew, under awakening skies.

Heart of gold, a sanctuary in the scorching heat,
A shade from life's relentless beat,
A shrine of purity, untouched and full of grace
All my troubles disappear with your embrace.

So sweet and gentle, your presence divine,
In your love's encompass, my life becomes sublime
For you're the dream every soul longs to find,
A beacon of love, gentle prayer forever with you I
bind.

In the silent depths of a tear-stained night,
Dreams for a few are a haunting sight.
I see their rainbow hearts conceal their soul,
I hear tales of rejection from a world that's cold.
I feel for the hearts, that are a canvas of colours bold,
Yet, forced to conform to Pink and Blue, a narrative ages old.

I share those tears, a river of pain, full of fear,
For the ones they've lost, the ones whom they held
so dear.
Their identity, a question, forever shrouded.
They search for acceptance, for a love that's true,
But in the societal chains, their freedom subdued.

In the shadows, they silently speak and weep,
In this world of binaries, they're lost and alone,
They confide the love denied, the secrets that are
heavy to keep.

A third dimension, that's often overthrown.
Their cry for recognition, echoes through time,
Let's hear the plea for humanity to redefine.
It is not only their pain, it's also yours and mine
Rainbow of dreams, like fragile petals, crushed,
In a world where they are not accepted but hushed.

Their pain, a whisper, that echoes through time,
A cry for recognition is a plea for a crime.

Yet in their tears, a resilience gleams,
Strength is born from the darkest streams.
The rainbow gets bigger, with every tear drop it does
rise;
One day they'll be treated like the rest, a hope gleams
in their eyes.

The search for identity, a journey so long,
A path that's winding, where self is said to be wrong.
It's a call for recognition, acceptance, and love.
Urging to pave the path to a kinder fate.
Pink and Blue is not the only mate
Give everyone the freedom to choose
Rainbow of dreams, don't have to gather the strength
to try
To bloom anew beneath the vibrant sky.

Life

Life is not what you pass by,
But what you live, as moments fly.
Life is not just what you see,
But what you feel, deep within, like the buzz of a bee.

Life is not just what you hear,
But what you understand, so clear.
Life is not just what you get,
But when you try your best, with no regret.

Life is not just what you think,
But all what happens, in a blink.

Life is only one and waits for none,
Don't let it slip before you are done.

Live it fully, feel each part,
Understand it with all your heart.
Try your best and seize the day,
Enjoy each moment, come what may.

Let Me Free

51

The call of the green tree
Whispers to me to set free.
Birds in the high sky
Invite me to come and fly.

The sun, shining bright,
Guides me toward the path of right.

The tree of life, the bird of freedom,
The sun's energy—all my kingdom.

That's who I was, that's who I am,
That's who I will always be.

Calls of relations,
Bonds of nations
Do not bind me—I am free.

I am an evergreen tree,
I am an eagle, soaring free.
Let me be me, I am not meant for thee,
In the blue sky and heavens high.
Let me try, let me fly.

I Did It

I walked through the woods,
Deep, dark, and scary,
All by myself, as fast as I could,
The journey left me weary.

Oh, I can't take another step,
But I had to move, I had to go.
I screamed in helplessness,
Only to hear my echo.

Should I give up, should I stop?

If I did, I'd surely be lost and gone
In this world, deep, dark, and scary.
I gathered my courage and pressed on.

I crossed rivers, groves, weeds, and thorns,
Facing dusky skies and raging waters.
Fighting through the deadly briers,
I walked and walked, with tireless desire.

I had almost crossed the woods,
Deep, dark, and scary.
I took a deep breath, the scent of roses revived me.
I opened my weary eyes and saw the shining light.
As far as my sight went, everything was green and
bright.
Bees, butterflies, rainbows told me that I survived.

Oh, I was spellbound by the beauty bright
I knew I would cross the jungle and reach the
prairie.
I had tried and toiled to witness this light.

Finally, I crossed the woods, deep, dark, and scary.

Now, I'm engulfed in the warmth of the bright day,
Enjoying the fruits of my sheer grit.
Blessed with colour beyond the gray,
I shout aloud with pride: I DID IT.

MA

You stride like Hercules, bold,
Yet your touch, tender as a buds unfold.
Your warmth, like the sun's bright boon,
Yet your gentleness rivals the tender moon.

With the fierceness of a lioness, you roar,
Protecting me, guarding my life's shore.
Yet you are as serene as dew in every sunrise,
Your heart whispered prayers, blessings and advise

You are my in life's raging storm,
Yet your love, a haven, gentle and warm.

Alas! the warmth of your embrace, now just a dream,
In all the corners, your laughter's silently stream.

In the hush of twilight's embrace, you are missed,
Your absence felt, memories kissed.
Your touch, a whisper in the evening breeze,
In the shadows where your presence flees.

In the aroma of my kitchen, your recipes remain,
A reminder of your love shall not wane.
Your absence is a void in my heart's fold,
Your spirit is a beacon though, keeps me strong and
bold.
Though you may be gone, your love endures,
Every moment, every memory, you reassure.
In every corner of my heart, I feel a trace of your
grace,
You live not only in my heart but in time and space.

His Presence

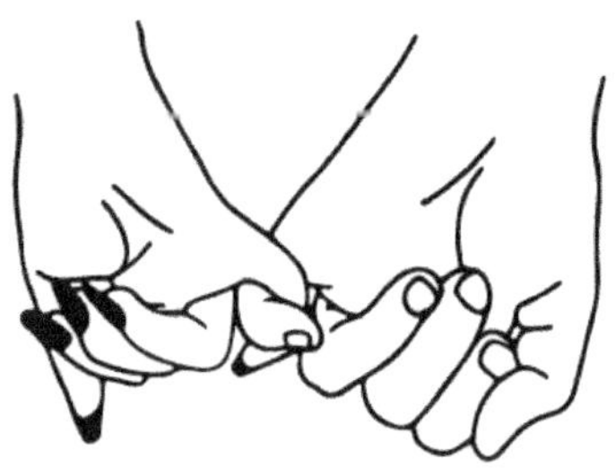

In the quiet corners of my soul, he dwells,
His love, a silent river, runs in me deep and true,
A man of few words, but a heart that swells.
In his gestures small, he whispers, "I love you."

In everyday moments, he's always there,
Though not adorned with artful speech,
Showing his affection with thoughtful care.
His actions speak volumes, beyond reach.

His words may stumble, his gestures small,
He may not declare with grandiose flair,

But in his heart, love stands tall.
Yet his care, like a gentle prayer.

In the rhythm of our everyday life as a pair,
The chores he shares, the burdens he readily bears,
In his own quiet ways, he shows his care,
Proves his care for me, as he silently declares.

With quiet strength, he stands by my side,
For in his quietude, love is found,
In every storm, I found him aside.
In every silence, his love is profound.

Jen!!!

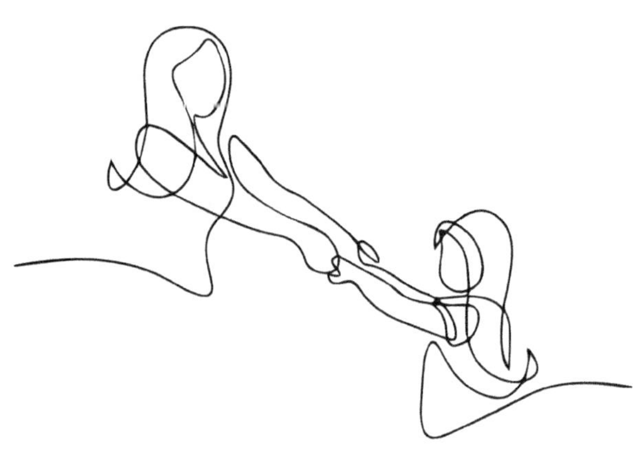

O' radiant star that dawned in my life, in you, I find my truest part.
A gem more precious than diamond or emerald,
Your presence, your melody, always fills my heart,
You are the symphony of love and hope that fills my world,
You are the sun that lights up my days,
The moon that soothes my nights with grace,
Your dimpled smile, makes my pains erase,
In your hugs, I find an eternal embrace.

In your journey, I see a story beautifully unfold,
With each step you take, my heart prays that you excel,
I'm filled with pride, when I see your spirit strong
and bold,
Your spirit will guide you, where dreams dwell.

Grow, my love, with strength and delight,
Face the world with courage, vigour and light,
In your hands, you hold the world's commands
As you grow, my pride expands,

May your dreams soar beyond the horizon,
Your spirit as free as the open sky,
My precious girl, my shining sun,
Know that I'll be here, by and by,

For in you, my love, I see the divine,
A miracle of life, forever enshrined,
My daughter, my joy, my eternal sunshine,
With your glow, my world is perfectly aligned.

Jen, you are, my treasure, my gift from above,
You're my sunshine, my joy, and always my little
one,
In your warmth, I find love, and my battles are
won.
In you, I've discovered the true meaning of love.